DEFYING THE STORMS IN YOUR LIFE

DEFYING THE STORMS IN YOUR LIFE

How to overcome the problems in your life and even make history

Richardson George

ACKNOWLEDGEMENTS

All praise to God for His abundant grace in enabling me to write this inspirational and motivational book. It was an actual storm named Bret which struck Trinidad and Tobago in June 2017 that God used to inspire the writing of this book to provide practical principles for us to more effectively face and defy the storms in our lives. Additionally, I wish to express sincere gratitude to:

My precious wife, Libby George for her assistance in proof reading the manuscript for this book despite her busy schedule.

Mrs. Euline Peters and Mrs. Hazel Gobin also for their assistance in proof reading the manuscript.

Mr. Justin Zephryn for his assistance in the final editing of the book.

Rev. Dr. Benjamin Agard, the National Director of the Open Bible Standard Churches of Trinidad and Tobago, Inc. for availing himself to write the foreword of this book.

The members of the Claxton Bay Open Standard Church of which I am currently the senior pastor and at which I originally shared many of the principles contained in this book.

Contents

FOREWORD

The author of this book, *"Defying the Storms in Your Life,"* Rev. Richardson George, is a developing author whose work which includes, *"Developing Dynamic Disciples"* (English & Spanish), *"That Will Never Happen To Me,"* *"Great Commission Christians"* and *"Living The Overcoming Life"* is becoming more and more valuable to his growing audience.

This latest release speaks to the issue of adverse experiences in life and provides principles on how to address them. Storms happen to everyone regardless of age, race, marital status, financial standing, time serving the Lord or any other circumstance. The author generously shares his own experiences of defying those storms faced by him and his family. As he delves into Peter's response to his storm, the author puts a positive spin on this history-maker who, to date remains the only person who has ever walked on water. We can also make history through our rich experiences if we are willing to listen to and obey the voice of the Master as Peter did so courageously. I am sure you will add value to your life as you practice the principles Rev. George has released in his book, "Defying the Storms in Your Life."

WHY YOU SHOULD READ THIS BOOK

On 13th September 2008, the devastating category 2 hurricane Ike pounded the town of Gilchrist, Texas with such fury that it left a trail of destruction in its path. Residents were left traumatized at the widespread devastation. Every single house within a few blocks was flattened by hurricane Ike except one house owned by Warren and Pat Adams. Their house remained standing tall after the hurricane had come and gone (Wafflesatnoon, May 14, 2016). Remarkable! This house, in effect had defied hurricane Ike. This resistant house proves that regardless of the severity of a life storm and the many people who may collapse under its impact, you can certainly defy it and stand tall.

This book focuses on the account of a storm at sea recorded in Matthew 14:22-33. The disciples of Jesus were caught in this severe storm while sailing across the Sea of Galilee and Jesus went to them walking on the water. After some verbal exchanges with Jesus, Peter actually walked on the water then began to sink. As I reflect on past expositions of this passage, I realize that we tend to focus more on Peter sinking rather than on him walking on the water. Most times I hear an exposition on this passage, the message highlights Peter's mistake of taking his eyes off Jesus and as a result of this, sinking. This is followed by an exhortation to keep our eyes on Jesus if we want to avoid sinking. While this serves a useful purpose, it is a somewhat limited view of the passage which emphasizes Peter's failure rather than his success. Few people sharing on this passage expound on Peter's successful walk on water in the midst of a violent storm. Most people minimize and sometimes overlook that salient fact entirely. This happens because it is natural for human beings to focus on negatives and failures rather than on positives and successes. In some way, we may be predisposed to operate this way.

For an ordinary man to walk on water was an achievement that had never been done before and has never been repeated since. Yet that achievement has been slighted in preference for his sinking. On that day Peter defied a life threatening storm and also made history. Such an accomplishment must be acknowledged and celebrated. Not only that, but the account should be examined closely to extract from it some very valuable life principles to apply when we face our personal storms.

Peter did several specific things and observed some specific principles that enabled him to walk on the water and defy the storm that day. If we discover those principles and practice them, we too can walk on water defying the fierce storms in our personal lives and even make history.

On a more personal level, have you ever noticed that some people focus on problems rather than on possibilities and solutions? They are problem oriented rather than solution oriented. They tend to see the problem in every proposed solution. Such people generally seldom defy storms in their lives and never make history because they are trapped and defeated by their own problem mentality. On the other hand, people who defy the storms in their lives view situations differently, thus positioning themselves to even make history in some way as Peter did.

Peter never thought and didn't know that he was going to make history that fateful day when his personal history was about to come to an abrupt end. Nevertheless, he defied the storm and made history that day inspiring future generations to face their storms confidently knowing that they can defy them and make history also.

Admittedly, just as storms or hurricanes of different strengths strike nations and wreak havoc with varying degrees of severity often leaving a trail of destruction behind them, so too, storms strike our lives from time to time with different degrees of intensity and consequent damage. Storms of any kind and of any intensity are always unwelcome. The reality though is that they do come, and when they strike we must be prepared for them.

The occurrence of a storm does not automatically spell destruction and devastation. For example, in 2017, while in St. Lucia with my son on vacation, a storm named Harvey was forecast to hit the island on Friday 18th August. In response, I prayed a simple prayer saying, "Lord, you didn't bring us to St. Lucia to face a storm so I ask you to intervene and do something in your own way in Jesus' name." That was the day prior to the forecast strike date.

We prepared ourselves by going indoors. However, sleep seemed to have remained outside for a considerable time longer than we did. Lying restlessly on the bed, until long after midnight, I heard strong winds howling as they forced their way through cracks and crevices in the building. From occasional glimpses outside, I observed the surrounding trees swaying vigorously in the breeze as Harvey struck. After approximately twenty minutes, the trees regained their composure and sleep entered the room to be reunited with me.

The next day, the nation was on high alert with everyone expecting the worst. All businesses including those at the hotel were closed by order of the government. Between 12 noon and 1:00 pm was the predicted time of disaster. We waited passively all morning observing the trickling rain, but it was while having lunch, the activity picked up. The rain was now intensified and the trees were again agitated by the ferocious winds as we looked on in dismay. To our delight, this fury only lasted approximately five minutes in my estimation. That day the storm struck St. Lucia but there was no devastation as expected, and people were left dumbfounded wondering what had happened.

Later that week the same hurricane travelled to Texas and wreaked unprecedented havoc causing history-making floods where roads became rivers. St. Lucia though, defied the storm miraculously that day. This shows that destruction is not an automatic outcome when a storm strikes. Storms can be defied, so you can face confidently the unavoidable storms that strike your life and defy them.

Have you ever felt like you are in a category 5 storm and you don't know what to do? Do you feel like giving up, checking out, calling it quits, resigning, closing up shop, bursting under the pressure, killing yourself, killing somebody, running away, giving up on God or doing some other regrettable thing? Then this book is just for you.

Unfortunately, life is like a constant hurricane season requiring a state of perpetual preparedness because we never know when a storm will develop and strike. Therefore, as you read this book, be prepared to learn and apply the storm defying principles outlined so you can confidently defy the storms that strike your life. At the same time, you will be exposed to the real possibility of being a history-maker.

On 20th June 2017 Trinidad and Tobago was struck by Tropical Storm Bret. According to the National Hurricane Center Tropical Cyclone Report (5th March 2018), this was the second for the hurricane season in the Caribbean and is on record as the earliest named storm in the region In the aftermath of storm Bret, in comparison with the other storms that struck the Caribbean region in 2017, one quickly realizes that the damage done to Trinidad and Tobago was minimal compared to the devastation experienced by other countries. To a large extent and for various reasons, Trinidad & Tobago was able to withstand and in some respects defy the storm Bret.

Storms and hurricanes have become commonplace in the Caribbean. They are unavoidable and highly unpredictable in the fury they unleash upon countries in their path. So too, in the journey of life, storms of unpredictable strength strike us, often unexpectedly and sometimes threaten to destroy us. To unsuspecting and unprepared persons such storms of any category can devastate them and leave them in shambles with little hope of recovery. These storms are not associated with the weather but have the potential to inflict great damage and even kill just like natural storms. However, destruction and death are not automatic outcomes when a storm strikes. Like the house that remained standing when all others collapsed after the storm passed, defying the storms in your own life is a real possibility when you know what to do and actually do it. *You can defy the storms in your life.* I wrote this book to let you know that you can defy every storm that beats against your life and remain standing tall when the howling winds cease and the life-threatening flood waters subside.

At this time, let me define the concept of "defy." Firstly, I want to mention how the word defy is not used. Defy is not used in a negative sense to mean rebel or disobey. Rather, as used throughout this book, the word defy means to do something considered impossible; to confront with assured power of resisting (Merriam-Webster online dictionary); to resist completely in a baffling way (Webster's New World Dictionary: Second College Edition). In my words, to defy means to face something bigger than yourself and defeat it or get the victory over it. It is expected that storms will strike your life, but when they come, you can most certainly defy them.

In the Gospel according to Matthew 14:22 – 33, Jesus had just performed a mighty miracle of feeding 5,000 men with five loaves of bread and two fishes. After sending the crowd away, Jesus told the disciples to go to the other side of the sea which they did. When they reached the middle of the sea i.e.

approximately 3½ miles inside the 7 miles wide Sea of Galilee (Collier's Encyclopedia, 1983) a storm arose and threatened to kill everyone in the boat. However, some time after, they saw a figure approaching on the surface of the water. Unsure of what it was, they panicked and lamented their double calamity of a storm and now a ghost. It turned out that the figure was Jesus walking on the water; something the disciples never saw before and was naturally cautious in their response. A conversation ensued and at the end, Peter ended up doing the unthinkable when he actually walked on the water to go to Jesus in the midst of the raging storm. That day Peter defied the storm that threatened to terminate his life. Peter actually walked on the stormy sea that threatened to kill him. Like the disciples in Matthew 14, storms of one kind or another strike every person including me and you at one time or another during our lifetime and like Peter, you too can defy your storms.

CHAPTER 1

THE REALITY OF STORMS

As stated earlier, storms are an inescapable reality of life that we all have to face at some time. To think that you are exempted from experiencing storms in your life is to really be living in a fantasy world. In Matthew 14:15 – 21, Jesus had just performed a mighty miracle by feeding 5,000 men beside women and children with 5 loaves of bread and 2 fishes. Immediately after, Jesus told the disciples to *"go unto the other side"* of the Sea of Galilee while He sent the multitudes away (Matthew 14:22). A strange command? Apparently not. It was evident that they obeyed Him and set sail.

After smooth unperturbed sailing for a considerable period of time, they reached half way across the sea. Then Matthew tells us that *"the ship was now tossed with the waves; for the wind was contrary"* (Matthew 14:24). Other translations refer to the ship as a boat which word I will use throughout this book. The sea became turbulent reaching storm proportions. Whether the disciples experienced that before, the Bible does not say, but it is safe to say that they did not expect such a ferocious storm or they would not have ventured on that journey in the first place.

That storm was totally unexpected. However, the Sea of Galilee is known for the development of sudden storms despite previously calm weather (New Bible Dictionary 404). Meteorologists today can predict the development and advancement of a storm with a high degree of accuracy well before its appearance through contemporary, sophisticated weather-tracking equipment. Notwithstanding, some storms strike unexpectedly, as those on the Sea of Galilee which the disciples were experiencing that day. We call them "freak storms" today. As in the natural weather patterns, so too in life, storms of both types, predictable and unpredictable strike us, some of which we are better prepared for than others. While some people are caught off guard, many people defy and survive their storms. If they can, why can't you?

Are you facing a storm of some kind in your life right now? Is your storm relational; concerning your husband, wife, children, parents, friend, boyfriend, girlfriend, an 'ex' or some other relationship? Is it financial, spiritual, demonic, physical, mental (negative, destructive or suicidal thoughts dominate or plague your mind), educational or social? Is your storm caused by someone else like an alcoholic or abusive family member, an unfaithful spouse, a substance abuser in your family, your boss, a co-worker, a teacher, a neighbour, a political personnel, a leader you know or people you are leading? Then what follows in this book will definitely be very helpful to you in defying those storms in your life.

Sometimes a storm strikes when you least expect it, even immediately after a great victory. But don't be surprised or destabilized by the turn of events. Some people get consumed by a storm simply because they believe they should never experience problems. They wrongly believe that experiencing a storm is evidence that they are living in sin or doing something else horribly wrong. This is not true. Storms strike people as committed to Jesus as the disciples were so don't be surprised if you experience storms in your life. Never submit to the fury of your storm though because you can overcome your storm through Jesus Christ.

STORMS AND THE WILL OF GOD

People sometimes wonder if it is possible to be in the will of God and in a storm at the same time. The main text addresses this dilemma. The fact that Jesus said to the disciples *"Go unto the other side"* (vs 22) and they obeyed Him means that they were in the will of God when they set sail. It stands to reason that when the storm struck, the disciples were in the will of God because they were obeying an explicit instruction given by Jesus Himself. That is astounding, being in the will of God and experiencing a problem at the same time. Can that really happen? Yes, indeed.

Some people think that being in the will of God immunizes them against storms and negative experiences in life. Wrong. They assume that once they are in the will of God and doing what they know God wants them to do that no negative, unpleasant or even potentially destructive thing can happen to them. Some take this erroneous belief even further to state the opposite which is, if you are having bad, negative or unpleasant experiences then you are obviously out of the will of God. The unwanted, unfavourable experience is viewed as the consequence of or even judgment for something sinful that was committed. For such people, "displeasure is evidence of disobedience." Surely sin always produces bad consequences, but having bad experiences does not always mean that sin is the cause.

Don't be surprised, disturbed, discouraged or depressed when you are doing the will of God and something negative or even terrible happens. Once you are certain that sin is not the cause, then just remain faithful and keep on doing the will of God and pleasing Him. Even when you have no logical explanation for your unpleasant experience, remain faithful and true to God. Never come to a negative conclusion or take negative action based on negative experiences you don't understand. When you don't understand, it is better and even safer to do nothing than to do the wrong thing. Many people have violated this simple principle by taking impulsive wrong actions and end up suffering unnecessary negative consequences which they could have avoided. Today some of them are alcoholics, drug addicts, sexual perverts, insane, in prison, in mental institutions, living in regrettably unplanned domestic situations and a host of other undesirable situations.

Some have recovered from such adverse circumstances but learned the principle the hard way. Others are still suffering from the wrong actions they took because they misunderstood what being in the will of God implies. They thought erroneously that being in the will of God or even at the centre of

God's will meant living a problem free life, but that is not true. Certainly being in the will of God is the best place anyone can be, but it can also be accompanied by problems, even a storm as experienced by the disciples. Even Jesus Christ Himself experienced many negative circumstances in His life and overcame them. Therefore, when you are experiencing storms in your life, you should never be thrown off balance, question God, fly in the face of God or take wrong actions which you will later regret. Rather, keep your head on, remain faithful, exercise patience and believe God to bring you through your storm in His way.

When I got married I was excited about the prospect of starting a family of my own. When the time came to include children in the family, we waited for the birth of our first baby, but that did not happen. Six years after marriage my wife conceived and the baby was lost through a miscarriage. The journey to pregnancy continued year after year, but nothing happened. Ten years went by and no baby came. More years rolled by and barrenness persisted. It was now fifteen years and nothing. It was after sixteen years of marriage, countless consultations and explored alternatives that my wife Libby gave birth to a long awaited bouncing baby boy who we fondly referred to as our miracle baby.

To us that experience was a storm. Can you imagine how long those years were and what kinds of thoughts were racing through our minds and how much our emotional stability was tested? For all those years we were in the will of God even planting a new church. With God's help, we continued faithfully in ministry as we trusted God to undertake for us in this situation. We determined that whether God gave us a child or not, we will remain faithful to Him. That's an account of just one of the storms we faced and defied. What storm are you facing while you know that you are in the will of God? Don't give up. The disciples were the closest people to Jesus while on earth and He gave them an instruction which they obeyed and ended up in a storm. Suffice it to say that the disciples were in a storm and in the will of God at the same time.

Verse 24 tells us that when the storm struck *"the ship was now in the midst of the sea."* As if the storm itself wasn't bad enough, they were now in the middle of the sea which was the furthest point from help of any kind. With no help in sight, the situation seemed hopeless. To understand the seriousness of the situation, you must know that the Sea of Galilee was seven miles wide. To be in the middle of that sea meant that they were approximately three and a half miles from the shore and the depth could have been as much as 150 feet (Collier's Encyclopaedia, Vol. 10, 542). In that situation, they most likely did what came naturally which was to save themselves by bailing as much water out of the boat as possible. This was a life threatening storm, and remaining alive was their highest priority.

Life for us today is sometimes like the disciples caught in a storm with nowhere to turn for help. When we find ourselves in such a difficult situation we find it is then compounded by some other uncontrollable factors. It then becomes more difficult to escape from the situation than originally thought.

Our emotions run wild and despair sets in. Suicidal thoughts even take a jab at your mind aiming to deliver a fatal blow.

Maybe, right now you are in a situation that seems hopeless and you are wondering what to do. You are thinking about giving up or even killing yourself. I don't know what specific problem you are experiencing right now, so I cannot prescribe an action here that will apply to all of you who are reading this right now. However, I can tell you immediately what not to do and it is this - **DO NOT GIVE UP!** Giving up was never a solution in the past and it is not one now. Giving up is not an option.

Help came eventually and the disciples were delivered because they were still alive in the boat to experience the deliverance. They did not give up by jumping into the sea or doing some other erratic thing. How many people jump into the sea and end it all canceling their chances of deliverance. Don't be one of them. Believe God to come through for you as He did for the disciples. Continue reading and discover what you can do to defy the storm you may be experiencing right now.

Verse 24 tells us that the disciples were experiencing contrary winds and tossing waves in the unexpected storm. The situation was getting worse. Nothing unusual. In life, it is not strange for contrary winds and tossing waves to beat against us as the disciples experienced while being in the will of God. Some wrongfully assume that people in the will of God and even people in key positions of spiritual leadership should never experience adversity and if

20

they do, it is a sign of failure or weakness of some kind. The reality is that we face problems of many kinds in life. Some can become easier to bear or more complicated and difficult to bear with time. When the problem intensifies, all kinds of thoughts go through your mind, mostly negative, of course. Nevertheless, the final outcome after the storm depends upon your actions to a large extent. The way you respond to your problem is one of the most important factors if not the most important factor in determining how the situation ends. How you choose to respond will determine whether you will defy your storm or be defeated and destroyed by it.

What are you doing in the storm you are experiencing right now? Are you doing something that will make the situation worse or something that will improve your situation and bring you out of the storm? You may not be responsible for the storm, but you are certainly responsible for the actions you take while in the storm. I encourage you to take the right action and you will be happier by the results you will get than if you take the wrong action. Yes, do the right thing and you will be pleasantly surprised by the outcome. Something happened out in the open sea that averted a disaster and at the same time created history, but details of exactly what happened out there will follow later in the book.

At this time though, the disciples were still out at sea and naturally terrified because they were caught in this unpredicted storm in the middle of the sea; the waves were now contrary and the boat was being tossed to and fro. We are then told that all of this was happening *"In the fourth watch of the night"* (vs. 25) i.e. between 3:00 am and 6:00 am. What a time to be caught in a storm! This was the darkest period of the night when visibility was at its lowest and potential helpers were at their deepest in sleep.

Can you imagine the mental torture of the disciples frantically emptying water from the boat now being beaten from wave to wave as it sank deeper and deeper into the voracious ocean with each passing minute soon to disappear beneath its surface? That certainly looked like a helpless and hopeless situation, but fortunately, the experience did not end there with a wreck and mysterious disappearance of twelve men at sea. What appears to be certain doom, death and disappearance does not have to end that way and does not always end that way for many people. You can be one of them. Many people have passed through life storms as fierce as this one and even worse and defied them and so can you.

Sometimes when it rains it pours. Just when you think things would get better, they get worse. If it had not been a hopeless situation before, it definitely appears to be so now. Imagine experiencing a severe illness and while recuperating, you are fired, then a close family member gets in a serious accident a short while after, followed by the unexpected death of a parent or child. That is catastrophic.

The reality of life is sometimes like that where a situation deteriorates from bad to worse when all hope seems to be gone. Such complicated situations vary from person to person. Storms come in different categories. What do you do in such a situation when an unpredictable category 5 storm strikes your life? Do you give up or do you still hold on and hope and trust in God to deliver you? Remember, you always have options even when life gets so complicated, senseless and unbearable. You always have options and giving up is not the one to take if you want to defy that storm in your life. Giving up never helps, but hope in spite of the seemingly hopeless situation keeps the door for deliverance open. That kind of hope in an impossible situation is often referred to as faith. Such faith, not in faith but in God always believes God for deliverance, and God honours such faith. In fact, you don't need faith when you can see the way out. If you can see your way out, then you can act on what you are seeing and you don't need faith. You need faith when you can't see your way and only God can see the way out and come through for you.

Before giving details of how this faith can work for you as it did for Peter, I must state emphatically that God is bigger than any storm you are experiencing right now. God is able to bring you out and make you stand tall in defiance of that storm in your life. Look beyond your storm by faith and see Jesus and He will show up to help you. You can begin by expressing your faith in words by saying, "God, I know that you are bigger than my storm and I trust you to intervene and deliver me, in Jesus' name."

CHAPTER 2

WHEN JESUS SHOWS UP

The disciples were now desperate and on the brink of drowning at sea without a trace of their disappearance. They faced certain death. With low visibility and high winds accompanied by pouring rain, all hope was gone. As they were about to resign themselves to their irreversible destiny of destruction, they looked in the distance and saw a blurred object approaching the boat becoming larger as it drew closer. Their spontaneous response was to cry out for fear saying, *"it is a spirit"* (Matthew 14:26). When they thought nothing else could go wrong, a ghost now appears to finish them off. The appearance of this "ghost" further compounded the situation. The Bible tells us that *"they were troubled"* (Matthew 14:26). This was a traumatic experience pushing them closer to the breaking point as they sank deeper into the sea… into apparent oblivion.

Life sometimes feels like that. To use another analogy, it feels like all it takes now is one straw to break your back. Storms, difficulties and pressures in life, especially when compounded, are emotionally taxing and could cause you to break right before your deliverance comes. The thought of death crossed their minds, but it would not be death at their own hands.

While they contemplated the frightening outcome of their situation, the distant object kept drawing closer and closer. Fear intensified as hope diminished. The object drew closer and grew larger. Nevertheless, discerning the advancing object outside the boat was difficult due to the obscurity created by the storm conditions. Storms do that. They make it difficult to perceive accurately what is really happening in our immediate surroundings when we get caught in them. Storms make you feel as if the only reality right now is this storm, this problem. Our perspectives become distorted, our understanding is decreased, our ability to think rationally is reduced and our actions become erratic and unpredictable. This is why you have to take extreme care not to panic or overreact when you are experiencing a storm in your life because you might just do something or say something that you and possibly others will later regret.

The consolation is that no natural storm in history ever lasted forever. They all had a beginning and an end. However, when they struck, some people may have died, but the good news is that most people defied those storms and outlived them. They lived to tell their story. I encourage you to be someone who defies the storms in your life and live to tell your story to glorify God and to help others defy their storms.

The disciples' storm kept brewing and becoming more boisterous. Then suddenly, the disciples heard a distinct voice saying, *"Be of good cheer; it is I; be not afraid"* (Matthew 14:27). Those words were consoling, but their source was uncertain. With low visibility and loud background noise, the disciples were unsure of who it was that uttered those words. They subsequently discovered that it was Jesus who had come to their rescue walking on the water. WOW! What a timely appearance, on the brink of their breaking point. He revealed Himself to the disciples on the brink of death.

Jesus certainly knows how to come to our rescue when we are in need of Him most. That's why it is always a bad idea to give up when you are uncertain of the future, immediate or distant. Jesus will come through for you in His way and right on time. When you think that all hope is gone and any reversal in your situation is impossible, think again because Jesus specializes in showing up at such times. As the saying goes, "He may not be there when you want him, but he's always right on time."

The astonishing thing though is that although Jesus comes in time, He doesn't always come to our rescue the way we expect Him to. Because of this simple fact, we sometimes miss Jesus and also miss our opportunity for help and deliverance. We can have so many expectations of how God should show up for us and if He doesn't come as we expect, we run the risk of missing Him. Some people even try to tell God exactly how to help and deliver them, so if He shows up any other way, they miss their opportunity for deliverance and remain in their predicament.

Don't dictate to God how to answer your prayer and how to deliver you. Give God the freedom to show up however He chooses to. Give Him the freedom to do His thing His way. Give God the freedom to surprise you. So Jesus went to the disciples walking on the water. The disciples though thought they had seen a ghost and they were missing

God's intervention and their deliverance. They cried out for fear rather than shouted for joy. This totally unexpected appearance of Jesus triggered a totally unexpected response from the disciples, fear. The disciples were traumatized.

Watch out for fear. Fear is a killer. The number of people who died from fear cannot be calculated, but you don't have to be one of those people. If the storm didn't kill them, fear would have. They were troubled because of the unfamiliar and unexpected. The unfamiliar tends to trigger fear in our minds. Nevertheless, you can be assured in defying your storm because the Bible declares in II Timothy 1:7 that *"God hath not given us the spirit of fear; but of power, and of love, and of a sound mind."* The disciples didn't know that then, but you do now. Speak to your fear and say, "I reject you spirit of fear in the name of Jesus" and in so doing position yourself for the power of God to come into your situation to deliver you.

Do you know how many people miss God when He shows up? You don't have to miss Him. You have to learn to expect God to deliver you and even in the most unexpected way because He often does. Remember the Red Sea crossing - totally unexpected (Exodus 14). Who would have expected God to make a road in the middle of the Red Sea for the Israelites to walk through on dry ground? Unthinkable! Right, but not impossible. God is the God of the impossible and the unthinkable. You must always see God that way. You must always see God as the great God who specializes in doing the impossible. When Jesus shows up in your storm, believe Him to do something that might be humanly impossible but divinely possible. Believe Jesus for your deliverance.

CHAPTER 3

HOW TO DEFY YOUR STORM

As the storm raged externally, so raged the disciples' fear and uncertainty internally. Twelve helpless disciples trapped in a battered boat in a merciless storm with no way of escape. With the encouraging and seemingly baffling words *"Be of good cheer; it is I; be not afraid"* (Matthew 14:27) still ringing in their ears, the disciples remained in the "safety" of the boat.

Then suddenly, impulsive Peter blurted out, *"Lord, if it is you...tell me to come to you on the water"* (Matthew 14:28, NIV). What was Peter thinking? Did he see someone do that before? Did he learn that on YouTube? Was Peter in his right mind? What was really happening here? What was he trying to do? Peter was actually challenging the status quo, the normal, the expected response in a situation like that. The other disciples were thinking about death, but not Peter. While the other disciples were thinking about sinking; Peter was thinking about floating. Do you know that in some terribly difficult situations in life, most people think more like the other disciples and not like Peter? Their minds tend to be flooded with negative thoughts of failure, loss, termination, hopelessness and even death. They focus on impossibilities rather than on possibilities. Peter on the other hand was a possibility thinker. His statement revealed that he was willing to do or even try something that he had never done or seen anyone do. He was positioning himself to defy that storm.

HAVE DEFIANT FAITH

How does someone actually defy a storm? Defying your storm begins with a defiant faith in God. Defiant faith in God helps you to assess the situation from a divine perspective. While the storm was still raging, Peter made a courageous statement indicating that he was willing to exercise bold and even reckless faith despite the uncertainty of the outcome if he tries to go on the water. He was not sure of how it will turn out, but he was willing to take that risk and step out in faith. Peter's demonstrative faith set in motion something positive if not externally, at least internally. It did something in his heart that gave him the motivation not to accept defeat and death passively but to step out in faith believing God for deliverance. Exactly how that deliverance will come, he had no idea, but he was willing to take a risk. Faith like that gets God's attention.

When experiencing a challenge, tragedy or disaster in your life, are you inclined to exercise faith in God, do your own thing or sit passively waiting for something to happen? Peter couldn't wait passively. He uttered something that appeared irrational even erratic when he said, *"Lord, if it is you, tell me to come to you on the water"* (Matthew 14:27 NIV). He really couldn't wait.

People who defy their storms do not just wait passively for something positive to happen. They exercise faith that makes something happen as Peter did. Some people never get their deliverance, breakthrough, empowerment or anything from God because they are waiting for 100% certainty before they try or do anything. You have to do like Peter. You have to make a statement of faith as Peter did or do something else to activate your faith. Peter made a statement that helped to neutralize the fear, doubt and despair that the other disciples were experiencing and tugging at his own heart. Defeatists are paralyzed by fear and other negative emotions. They remain stuck in their battered life's boat tossed and controlled by the negative circumstances of life when there is another reality of victory outside the boat awaiting them. They never say anything remotely close to what Peter said and they never experience anything remotely close to what he experienced. Nevertheless, I encourage you to do like Peter and take a bold step of faith to challenge yourself to say something positive or do something positive that seems impossible while facing your problem rather than remaining stuck in fear, doubt, despair and negativism where you are.

Peter demonstrated faith while still in his predicament. What does Peter's statement of faith imply? Peter's faith implies that:

➤ Faith does not accept a difficult situation as inevitable and hopeless.
➤ Faith looks beyond the natural.
➤ Faith looks beyond the present.

- Faith looks beyond what can be seen with the natural eye.
- Faith sees possibilities, not impossibilities.
- Faith sees the Lord as the source of deliverance.
- Faith sees itself in a better position while still in the unpleasant situation.
- Faith dares to believe God for what seems impossible.
- Faith takes action in spite of negative feelings.
- Faith is willing to attempt something never done before.

The faith that defies storms incorporates all the above, but it takes one act of faith to pull them all together. Peter did it. He pulled all these principles of faith together in one concise statement when he said, *"Lord, if it is you, tell me to come to you on the water"* (Matthew 14:27 NIV). You too can make one powerful, confident, bold statement of faith that is appropriate to your unique situation and see God come through for you as you defy your storm. What statement of faith can you make in defiance to your storm? Think about it. Such a statement of faith neutralizes or cancels every opposing and faithless thought. Such a statement of faith prepares and positions you to defy your storm and remain standing tall when it blows over.

GET A WORD FROM GOD

It was after Peter expressed his bold faith and willingness to do something that had never been done, Jesus said to him *"Come"* (verse 29). He now had a choice. We always have a choice to either remain stuck, bound, defeated, overcome by our storm or to defy it. What Peter declared in faith was now tested, but the word of Jesus was reassuring to him although the storm was still raging. Peter got a word from God as it were. When you are experiencing a storm in your life, you need to get a word from God. It is great to know that God has a word for every situation including yours right now, you must get that word. God is not limited to one means of speaking to us. We cannot dictate to God exactly how He should give us that word when we need it most.

In fact, there are several means by which one can get a word from God. Like Peter, you can hear His voice audibly. This is what you hear with your physical ears. You can hear God's inaudible voice speaking to you internally. You do not hear words with your physical ears, but you get a clear message from God that you understand within your heart. God can speak to you through someone else whether through counsel, prophetic utterance or in some other way. God often uses other people to bring His message to us. Those people are not always known to us but are sometimes complete strangers. On occasions, the message comes almost accidentally through a chance encounter, but what appears to be accidental is really God orchestrating everything to deliver His word to you.

Finally, you can hear God's voice by reading His Word, the Holy Bible. This is the most common means by which God speaks to His people because

God can use this means to speak to us daily if we read His Word daily. Therefore, in your pursuit to get a word from God, begin by reading God's Word with an open heart to hear what He is saying to you before you take action. On a regular basis you should be reading the Bible one book at a time or studying specific topics of interest to you. Pay close attention to what God is saying to you as you read and study His Word. This list, however, is not a complete list of ways in which God can speak to you. Never limit God to come through for you only in your pre-determined way.

Jesus went to the disciples walking on the water. I wonder if Peter was the only one who believed it was Jesus walking on the water or did the other disciples have the same belief? If they did, they didn't give any evidence of belief or faith as Peter did. Some people miss their deliverance not because it is not available or impossible but because they have no active faith and do not know how to or do not make the effort to get a word from God. Peter heard the word of Jesus, *"Come"* and he responded positively. How do you respond when God is speaking to you, or get the distinct impression that God is saying something to you? Are you eager to act as Peter was or do you generally respond with hesitation? I urge you to take God's Word seriously and respond to it positively. Be ready to act when He speaks.

I remember being in a situation involving a strained relationship with someone and was not sure what to do. However, while reading Philippians 2:2, I received a clear answer from God saying *"having the same love."* This meant to me that I should still extend love to the person despite the emotional pain I was feeling. I did it and defied that storm which was brewing.

Unfortunately, some people have become so out of tune with God that they cannot decipher what He is saying when He speaks. It sounds like a foreign language to them. If that describes you, then you have to get back in tune with God. If you never had such a personal relationship with God, then get in touch with Him now for the first time, hear His voice and do what He says to you (You can pray the prayer on page 60 and mean every word as you do). When you do, you will see what He will do. It will happen though AFTER you exercise bold faith and get God's Word. If you try to act prematurely you might be unpleasantly surprised by the outcome. If you could only get a quick fix without faith in God and His Word that will be great. That's not how it works though. You have to get those first. Peter had faith which predisposed him to act and a word from Jesus which provided the basis for his action. Peter didn't know it then, but he had something great awaiting him. He was putting things in place and preparing himself to defy his storm that day. God has something great awaiting you. Prepare yourself now and see what God will do for you.

TAKE ACTION

Jesus said to Peter *"Come."* Now it was Peter's move. He had faith and the word of Jesus in his heart. The storm still threatened death. Nevertheless,

Peter responded. He did the unthinkable, the unimaginable and seemingly impossible as described in these words, *"So Peter got out of the boat and walked on the water toward Jesus"* (Matthew14:29 God's Word). In that life threatening storm, Peter actually stepped out of the boat. He got his word from God *"Come"* and stepped out on it. The Bible does not tell us exactly how Peter got out of the boat; whether he hurried out, moved slowly and cautiously or jumped out is not stated explicitly. What is clear is that he got out of the boat boldly defying that storm. He was not going to allow the storm to kill him in the boat. It was not a suicidal act. He already had faith and God's word and then took appropriate action. In other words, Peter was obedient. Obedience speaks of positive action in response to an instruction.

What are you doing with the words you get from God? Do you just pile them up and wait for new words from God? Do you try to get a fresh word just for the sake of knowing something more or do you act on what you already know? The truth is that action brings results. Action speaks of obedience. It is when you step out and act on God's Word that you will defy and overcome the storms in your life. We sometimes underestimate the importance and impact of obedience.

What is obedience? Obedience means basically "to carry out an instruction" (Webster's New World Dictionary: Second College Edition). Sometimes the problem is not that God is not speaking but we are not obeying when He speaks. People who do not give in to the pressures and problems of life and remain standing tall after a severe storm hits their lives are not lucky but obedient to the Word of God. Obedience to God works and delivers every time.

In the storm that you are experiencing right now, are you being obedient to God? Are you doing what you already know God wants you to do right now? If yes, then you are obedient. Remain obedient. Obedience is not a matter of the action being easy or hard, convenient or inconvenient but about it being right and beneficial. Obedience is not always easy, but it is always right. Obedience pleases God every time and always works for you. Disobedience, on the other hand, displeases God every time and always works against you. In every storm, you have choices to make unless you are knocked totally unconscious. You have the choice to obey God or disobey Him. You have the choice to take negative action that will keep you stuck in the storm, to sit and do nothing and hope that the storm will blow away or to obey God and defy the storm. Of course, the best thing to do is to obey God's Word and defy your storm.

Peter was not sure of exactly what would happen when he stepped out of that boat into the raging storm, but he did nevertheless. Despite all the uncertainties surrounding what he did not know, he acted on what he did know. He knew that he had a word from God and that was enough for him to step out in faith. Peter was obedient. The storm was still boisterous, but he stepped out nevertheless. Are you waiting for the storm to calm down before you step out and trust God? Don't. Step out in faith now. Not blind faith but faith based on a definite word or clear direction from God as Peter had. You will never know or experience what God has waiting for you until you step out. Stated differently, you will only know and experience what God has waiting for you when you step out in faith. Your responsibility is to get God's word and step out in faith. When God gives you His word, you can almost hear Him saying to you, "Your move now." You can move confidently because God always backs up His Word.

Do you remember when God instructed the children of Israel to go over the Jordan River into the promise land (Joshua 1:2)? At that time the Jordan River overflowed its banks spanning a breadth of one mile making it impossible to cross especially considering the women, children and babies in the camp (Unger's Bible Dictionary 605). Nevertheless, they had a word from God along with His promise of possession of the promise land. That was enough for Joshua. He had faith in God's word. Consequently, he motivated the people and did all the necessary preparation for crossing the river and entry into the promise land. The people were excited about the prospect of possessing their own land. However, it was only when their obedience was activated and the feet of the priests actually touched the water of the Jordan River that the flood subsided. The flow of the water was cut off, so they went over on dry ground (Joshua 3:15 - 17). They had a distinct word from God and an exciting faith that stimulated them to make the necessary preparations. However, it was only at the point of obedience to God that the breakthrough came. The Bible puts it this way, *"And as they that bare the ark were come unto Jordan, and the feet of the priests that bare the ark were dipped in the brim of the water ... That the waters which came down from above stood* and *rose up upon an heap very far from the city Adam, that* is *beside Zaretan: and those that came down toward the sea of the plain,* even *the salt sea, failed, and were cut off:..."*

Maybe you have been waiting for God to do something while He is waiting for you to do something. He has been waiting for you to make your move in obedience. Don't delay. You may be experiencing a storm of some kind right now, probably unemployment, prolonged frustrating singleness, unbearable marital problems, addictions, rejection, loneliness, fear, uncontrollable vices, severe relational problems, depression, obsession, confusion, an illness such as OCD, HPV, HIV, an incurable disease or a host of other things, and you have accepted the situation passively as being inevitable and hopeless. You think that there is nothing you can do about it. Not true. Think again. In every storm, God has a word for you regardless of the specific storm you are facing. Many people before you have experienced these storms and defied them in some way. You too can defy your storm. My encouragement to you is to get into God's Word and more importantly, get God's Word into you and step out on it! When God speaks to you, pay attention to what He says and obey Him. The truth is that obedience is the key to deliverance and defying your storm.

Is your life one of obedience or disobedience to God right now? If obedience, continue to obey God and be faithful to Him even if your storm has not disappeared as yet. Remember, victory isn't always as immediate as Peter's was and needed to be. The reality is that victory sometimes takes a little longer to come than we expect, so consistent obedience is necessary. If you are not living in obedience to God, then start now and position yourself to defy your storm. The fact is that there is no substitute for obedience. If you are obedient, it works for you. If you are disobedient, it works against you.

Storms in the natural can be very unpredictable, catastrophic and deadly. Unfortunately, the same is true of storms in our natural lives and even in our spiritual lives. You probably know people who used to have a strong spiritual life and today they are spiritually dead or badly wounded because they did not take positive action to defy the storms in their lives. I urge you though to take positive action and live a life of continuous obedience to God and He will give you the victory. When you stand on God's Word, He will stand by His promise. The Bible tells us about people who experienced the blessing of obedience:

1.   The Old Testament tells us about Naaman, commander of the Syrian army who was told by the prophet Elisha exactly what to do in order to be healed from his leprosy. He protested when he heard about washing seven times in the dirty Jordan River when there were so many other cleaner rivers in his homeland. Nevertheless, with some encouragement from his servants, he decided to wash in the dirty Jordan River as instructed. The instruction was very specific. Wash in the river seven times. Naaman began dipping, and you can imagine the apprehension as he dipped time after time with no visible results of healing. He looked at his body after the sixth time

and still nothing happened. One more dip. As Naaman plunged beneath the surface of the murky water the seventh time then sprang to his feet, he was amazed at the smooth texture of his skin now restored.

We see that it was when Naaman obeyed to the letter that God delivered him (II Kings 5:1 - 14 Amplified). When you obey, God will deliver you in His way.

2. The New Testament tells us about ten lepers who met Jesus on His way to Jerusalem and asked Him to have mercy on them. In response, Jesus said, *"Go show yourselves unto the priests."* We are told that *"as they went, they were cleansed."* It was when they obeyed, they were cleansed (Luke 17:11-16). God will come through for us also when we obey.

CHAPTER 4

THE STORM DEFIED

Peter stepping out of the boat but being unsure of what will actually happen became absolutely amazed when he realized that he did not sink but walked on the water. The Bible expresses it this way, *"So Peter got out of the boat and walked on the water toward Jesus"* (Matthew14:29 God's Word). At the precise moment of coming out of the ship and touching the surface of the swirling water, it became a solid pavement under Peter's feet and he walked on it to go to Jesus. That day Peter experienced an unprecedented miracle. It was beyond anything he could have imagined or expected, but the fact that he stepped out suggests that he expected something to happen. Something happened. He walked on the water, and that was beyond his wildest expectations. Peter made history that day.

Anybody, including you, can have such experiences, but unfortunately, some people will never experience anything like that. Any one of Jesus' disciples could have walked on water that day, but only Peter did. Anyone of them could have said what Peter said or did what he did, but they didn't. Not that they couldn't, but they simply didn't. If Peter could have done it, they could have done it also. Peter had nothing special going for him that they didn't have. Peter was not superior to them.

I sometimes try to imagine what the other disciples were doing while Peter was making history walking on water. I could almost see them bailing water out of the ship frantically trying to save themselves from sinking. Some were probably screaming in fear in the face of certain death. Some probably had their eyes fastened on Peter fearful of him going under at any moment while others were left with their jaws hanging from disbelief at the thought of a mere man walking on water. They probably looked on in shock as the drama of a normal human being walking on water unfolded. Emotions were probably running wild. They continued watching as Peter continued walking.

Whenever I reflect on this account and consider the frightened disciples in the ship, some questions come to mind for us today. Are you more like the disciples panicking in the boat or like Peter walking on the water? The other disciples watched on as Peter made history. The big question though is this, are you a history maker or a history-maker watcher? The other disciples were history-maker watchers while Peter was the history-maker. As stated previously, anyone of them could have made history that day. Anyone of us can make history today, and you can most certainly make history also if you are willing to do what Peter did. You can possibly make history that hits the Guinness Book of Records. You never know. Many people in that book didn't know that they would make history one day. When one thinks of making history, great outstanding international accomplishments like athletic feats, mind boggling discoveries and spectacular inventions come to mind. However, history-making does not necessarily have to be on such a large scale that receives worldwide acclaim or recognition.

You can make history in any sphere of life on a large or small scale. You can possibly make history on a hemispherical or regional level. If not, what about the national level? Yet on a smaller scale, some people make history for their community and many people are known to make history for their families. You can even make history in your organization, school, club, workplace or other group you are a member of? That being so gives you and everyone else the opportunity to make history in any sphere of society. Never tell yourself you cannot come out of your storm or even defy your storm while still in it. Like Peter you can defy your storm, and possibly make history.

The good news is that there is a big miracle awaiting you on the other side of your faith and obedience if you are willing to step out of your boat into the midst of the ferocious storm as Peter did. In other words, what positive action(s) are you willing to take to show that you have active faith in God and that you are willing to obey Him? Are you willing to do any of the following as well as other positive things not specified here to step out of your boat? Are you willing to:

➤ Pray and fast for your specific situation?
➤ Give a little more than you normally do?
➤ Show love to those you have a strained relationship with instead of taking revenge or avoiding them?
➤ Try to make peace with your enemies?

➢ Do something positive that people don't expect you to do in your current situation?

➢ Refuse to do something negative that people thought you would do if placed in the same situation?

➢ Do the exact opposite of the evil thoughts that Satan brings to your mind when you think about your problem?

If you are not willing to take positive action, don't be surprised if you remain stuck in your boat continuing to battle your storm and never come out of your situation walking on water. Do you really want to defy your storm, overcome your problem and experience a miracle? The truth is that you can defy your storm and overcome your adversity and difficulty if you act on God's Word and practice biblical principles. Therefore, get God's Word, take action and experience your miracle.

I want to say though that miracles happen when we have a need and believe God to meet that need. Miracles generally happen in response to problems. Miracles happen to deal with problems. Miracles happen as God's solution to problems. However, our thoughts, attitude, talk and actions reveal whether we really believe in God to help us to overcome the problem. They must all be harmonized to express our faith and obedience to God. Do not cancel your miracle by your negative thinking, attitude, talk or actions, but demonstrate by everything you say and do that you really believe God to meet that need and see Him come through for you.

The fact that Peter actually walked on the water revealed that there was harmony in his thinking, attitude, talk and actions. Remarkable! Peter defied the storm that day and made history at the same time. No man either before or after him is known to have walked on water. A death sentencing situation was transformed into a history-making adventure. What are the characteristics Peter demonstrated that made him a history-maker that day?

CHAPTER 5

CHARACTERISTICS OF HISTORY-MAKERS

The setting: The disciples were caught in a life threatening storm where death was certain. While doing all in their power to save their lives, a ghost-like figure appears in the distance heightening their fear and confirming their doom. To calm their fears, the figure spoke claiming to be Jesus saying *"Be of good cheer; it is I; be not afraid."* Quite spontaneously, Peter blurted out the words, *"Lord, if it be thou, bid me come unto thee on the water."* Jesus said one word, *"Come."* Without much contemplation or any hesitation, Peter stepped out of the boat and to everyone's amazement, he walked on the water and that day made history in the storm. Predictable tragedy was turned into glorious triumph.

Now, how does something like that happen? How did Peter take a storm and make history out of it? How does one do that?

Like this account in the Bible, many times making history is not planned but is a spontaneous response to a terrible situation, a severe problem, a tough challenge, a difficult test, a stiff competition, a pressing personal need, meeting someone else's need a seemingly lost cause etc. In the midst of such situations, people make history.

Sometimes life positions us ideally to experience a miracle or to make history, like being caught in an unexpected "storm" or being confronted by an unwelcome problem. When life is normal and the sea of your life is calm, there is no opportunity or necessity to do something out of the ordinary. It is extreme circumstances that provide the ideal opportunity for extraordinary creativity and for making history. Generally speaking, history makers are people who faced a problem of some kind that they were willing to put every effort into resolving and they succeeded. What are the characteristics of people who take such adverse circumstances and make history out of them?

The biblical account tells us that Peter was caught in a storm and made history in it. He walked on water. Although he was sinking momentarily which most people focus on and I have chosen not to, the account ends with Peter walking confidently on the water with Jesus back to the boat.

This section of the book on characteristics of history-makers focuses on making history in a storm like Peter did but is not limited to such severe circumstances. You don't have to wait for a storm to make history. People who make history do so under many different circumstances. This passage in Matthew 14:22 – 33 reveals several characteristics of history-makers that are very instructive to us. They can have universal application regardless of one's circumstances in life.

As we go through our unique life experiences, we have to make decisions and take certain actions that can become history making. Anyone willing to demonstrate these characteristics can be a history-maker in some sphere of life and most certainly, you too can be a history-maker if you are willing to follow these principles.

1. A history-maker is not hindered by what others do or don't do

People who make history do not depend on the action or inaction of others. They make history regardless of the involvement or non-involvement of others. Lack of support from others does not prevent such persons from making history. That is not to say that history makers never get support from others. Many times they do, but they are not hindered from venturing out when they do not get the support they expect from others. They take action despite what others do or don't do.

Peter made history despite the response of his fellow disciples. What were the other disciples in the same boat and storm doing? As mentioned previously, they were panicking and possibly bailing out water. What were they not doing? They were not stepping out of the boat in faith. Unfortunately, many people allow others to hinder them from making history, making progress or even achieving their personal goals in life. There are things within their power to do that do not depend on others, yet they don't do those things not because of inability but often because of the negative influence of others.

Peter had the option to allow his fellow disciples to influence him to do what they were doing, but chose otherwise by stepping out of the boat and walking on the water. People like that seem to be few. Not really. It could have been any one of them.

Why not you? Do not allow others to hinder you from making history or even from being what God created you to be and do.

2. A history-maker does not define himself by the limitations of others

The history-maker does not impose on himself the limitations that others have or have imposed on themselves. Key influencers in your life can have self-imposed limitations so that there are certain things they will never try and even discourage others from trying. You may have such people in your life. It could be anybody ranging from your closest family members to your most distant associate. Beware! Beware of others who try to impose their limitations on you and tell you what you can do and what you cannot do. If they succeed, they will influence you to define yourself by their limitations and to be able to do only what they can do. History-makers though, do not define themselves by the limitations of other people.

While bathing in one of the azure blue beaches in beautiful Barbados, my brother and his daughters swam out to a raft about 150 feet from the shoreline in fifteen to twenty feet deep water. I would never attempt that, but my son wanted to go. He was only ten years old and I naturally feared for him. After some thought, I said to myself that I should not restrict him because of my fear and limitation, so I told him to go. He had some prior swimming lessons in a swimming pool, but to my surprise, he swam the entire distance without stopping then stood on the raft waving triumphantly at me. Of course, I had my brother and two nieces strategically positioned around him, but they never touched him. That was a challenge for my son, but it turned out to be a victory and history-making moment for him.

The other disciples could have walked on the water that day but they were operating within their self-imposed limitations, so they remained in the boat. Just to use my imagination a bit, while Peter was talking to Jesus, they were probably telling him things to dissuade and discourage him from taking the action he eventually took. Nevertheless, Peter broke the limitation of the other disciples and made history walking on the water. When you are willing to transcend the limitations others try to put on your life, you will walk on water too. Don't tell yourself you cannot because others do not or cannot.

3. A history-maker takes risks that others are afraid to take

History-making always involves a risk. It involves doing something that you do not have concrete information on from personal knowledge, from research or from the experience of others you know. There are also many uncertainties about the outcome if you take certain actions. Because of these and other risk factors, most people never make history. Many people never make history not because they cannot but because they are afraid to take risks. They calculate too much. However, that is not to suggest thoughtless action or endorse stupidity.

I don't know how much calculation Peter did if any at all before stepping out of the boat into the water. The passage though suggests that Peter did not do any calculation. His action was spontaneous. When his foot touched the swirling water, he realized that he didn't sink but remained buoyant and was walking on water. It was worth the risk. Peter made history. He made history defying not only the storm but all human calculations. What risk are you afraid to take? What are you waiting for to step out? Go ahead.

4. A history-maker is willing to try something that nobody else ever did before

Making history in any given category implies that it was never done by anyone before or never done in that way or to that extent. Therefore, the person who makes history in a given category naturally does not have an example to follow or someone to give specific instructions on exactly how to do it before making history. Despite that, the history-maker is willing to try something without any evidence that it worked before. The history-maker who has a "strange" idea in mind, in any given situation, does not tell himself that it was never done before so he will not try it. No. Rather, he argues differently and says, "If nobody ever did it before, I will still try and I will, even if I have to be the first." He doesn't wait for evidence of it being done by others before he tries.

In the biblical passage, the storm was raging. Someone spoke from the storm claiming to be Jesus.

Nobody had evidence that it was Jesus. Then impetuous Peter blurted out, *"Lord, if it be thou, bid me come unto thee on the water."* He didn't question whether anybody before him ever did what he was asking. History shows that nobody ever walked on water before Peter did, but he was willing to try it nevertheless.

Maybe right now you have a word from God or an idea to do something you never heard someone else do before. Of course, all our actions must be consistent with biblical truth. What have you thought of trying that you never heard about before, or maybe never heard of in your country or in your given category? Now could be your time for action. Everything that exists and happens today was tried for the first time by someone who never saw it done before. In fact, everybody who accomplished great things or made history at one time tried it for the first time and most times failed at the first attempt. Ask Thomas Edison, the famous American inventor who after one and a half years of work developed the first incandescent light that was practical, safe and economical. Many others before him did not succeed (Edison Biography).

Do you know how many things some people could have done that they never did simply because they never tried? Do you have an idea that will be beneficial to others? Do you have an idea that could deliver you from your adversity? Do you have an idea that could even make history? Try it.

5. A history-maker overcomes fear of failure

Failure is always a possibility, but so is success. History-makers overcome fear and try because of the possibility of success. History-makers never allow the fear of failure to prevent them from trying. Failure is certain when not tried. Failure is not only defined by not succeeding in the attempt, but quite often failure is not trying at all. Failure to try because of the fear of failure is to deprive yourself of all the possibilities of success. It is often said that "It is better to try and fail than to fail to try." Much could be said and much has been said about fear, but my word of encouragement to you is to banish fear from your mind and take definite action to defy your storm and possibly make history at the same time.

When Peter stepped out of the boat and walked on the water, there wasn't the slightest trace of fear of sinking in his mind. We cannot say the same for the other disciples in the boat. No wonder they did not walk on the water. However, fear no longer has to prevent you from walking on that bad situation you are experiencing or from making history in your own sphere of influence. God has not given us the spirit of fear, but of power, and of love and of a sound mind (II Timothy 1:7)

6. A history-maker thinks outside the box

A history-maker is not bound to or confined by the thinking of others whether great or small, historical or contemporary, friend or foe. He thinks outside the confines of natural human thought and reasoning. As is commonly expressed today, a history-maker thinks outside the box. He thinks about things that never come to the minds of others without being heretical. He considers what others never do or are afraid to think about doing. He sees possibilities that appear far-fetched for the traditionalist and conservative. He sees beyond the horizon.

Peter was such a man. He had the composure and presence of mind to think outside the box even while undergoing the mental torment of being in a life threatening storm. In fact, Peter was not only thinking outside the box; he was thinking outside the boat. While all the others were seeing themselves dead inside the boat, Peter was seeing himself alive and walking on the water outside the boat. How can several people be in the same situation and see things so differently? How can people be in similarly bad situations and respond so differently? It is because of how they think. You can read more about our thoughts and thinking in my book Living The Overcoming Life: Practical Principles For Overcoming Life's Challenges. Peter was thinking differently from the other disciples. For Peter, there were possibilities outside the boat that were impossible inside the boat. Peter was willing to explore those possibilities outside and stepped out of the boat. While Peter was outside walking on the water making history, ALL the other disciples were inside the boat watching Peter make history.

While some people are overcoming and taking action to defy their storms, others remain stuck, neutralized and paralyzed by their storms. There is a solution to your problem, but it is outside the 'security' of your boat, your usual way of thinking, your usual way of viewing things, responding and doing things. God always makes a way of escape for you in your storm. He waits for you not just to think outside the box but to act outside the box. Change something and something will change. The action to take varies from person to person even within similar situations. I want to encourage you to pray for God's thoughts and direction and to act on one idea to defy your storm and not die in your boat.

7. A history-maker obeys the Word of God

Obedience to the Word of God is the key to victory in any situation. Much has been said about obedience already, but I just want to reinforce its importance in the context of history-making. Admittedly, not all history-makers have practiced biblical principles in doing so, but I encourage you to maintain a lifestyle of obedience to God's Word.

In the storm, Jesus said to Peter *"Come"* and immediately without hesitation, Peter obeyed and stepped out of the boat to go to Jesus. His positive response of obedience made him a history-maker. It is highly probable that your deliverance and victory in your storm is tied to your obedience to what God has said to you already, is saying to you now or will say to you in the future as you take time to listen to Him. Live a life of obedience and you will see what God will do for you.

8. A history-maker exercises faith

By this time you are convinced that if you want to defy your storm or even make history, you must not allow others to hinder you; you must overcome fear and take a risk; you must think outside the box and obey God in your situation. All these imply that you are ready to take action. As previously mentioned, whatever action you take though must be done in faith. Faith is based on the reliability of God and the expectation that He will intervene on your behalf. It is that unshakable confidence in your own heart that you are doing the right thing despite misunderstanding by others or lack of external confirmation.

Peter exercised faith when he stepped out of the boat into the water being fully aware that the normal expected consequence was to sink and of course drown because it was no calm swimming pool. To be in a difficult situation and take certain risky positive actions sometimes baffle faithless people who would not have done that if they were in the same situation. Some people in certain adverse circumstances would quicker use abusive or obscene language, pull out a weapon, give somebody a "piece of their mind" (no wonder some people are walking around like mindless zombies because they have given pieces of their mind to so many people), commit suicide or some other negative thing. They will never walk on water or overcome their problem like that, but not you. It really takes faith to take positive action when you are in a negative situation. In your problem, take faith action today that will help you to overcome and defy your storm.

9. A history-maker does not depend on others to follow him/her

Some people only take action when they have the support and backing of others. History-makers cannot afford to wait for others to follow them, so they don't. They take action when it is needed even if they have to go alone. They do not wait for followers before acting when they feel strongly impelled to take a certain course of action. This was evident when Peter stepped out of the boat into the ferocious storm without depending on anyone else to follow him. He did not wait for any pledge of support from his friends, not even a rope or life saver for safety, just in case. If you wait for others to follow you before acting in a particular situation or taking a step you have to take, you may never make a move and be stuck right there indefinitely. Sometimes that action is hard to take but necessary if you want to win over your situation and experience something which for you might be history-making. When you get a clear leading from the Lord as Peter heard Jesus say *"Come,"* you step out and take action, and don't wait for anyone to follow you.

10. A history-maker does not wait for 100% certainty before acting

Everything above says that if you will be a history maker in some sphere of life then you cannot wait for 100% certainty that what you want to do will be successful. History-makers do not wait for 100% certainty before acting. Some people have been waiting for something for years and they are still waiting today. Some people have refused to leave their community of birth, apply for a new job, get married, go for counselling, go back to school, start a business, start a new career, enter a rehab programme, write a book, compose a song, become a full time minister, get baptized, join a church, join a sports club, forgive an unremorseful offender and so many other things because they want to be 100% certain that they will succeed. People who defy their storms do not wait for 100% certainty that their plan of action will work. People who make history do not wait for 100% certainty that their idea or action will be accepted or succeed. Peter didn't wait for 100% certainty that the water will keep him afloat either before stepping unto it. Peter stepped unto the water in faith, walked on it defying his storm and making history that day. You can do the same before getting 100% certainty that you will succeed. I say confidently that you can defy the storms in your life and even make history. Yes, YOU. Go out and do it in Jesus' name.

Maybe you have read this entire book and benefited from the information shared in it about defying your storm and making history, but the Jesus that Peter responded to who eventually controlled the storm, you don't have a personal relationship with Him. I must say that the most storm defying and history-making event in my own life took place when I gave my life to Jesus Christ. Though young at the time, that commitment to Jesus was what really positioned me to live in victory over the storms I encounter in life today. It also helped me to overcome the uncertainty people have when they pass from this life into eternity. You probably never made that commitment to Jesus Christ, but if you never did, you can do it today and even right now by praying the following prayer and meaning every word of it.

PRAYER: *O God I acknowledge that I am a sinner and that I have done wrong things against you. I confess my sins and ask you to forgive me of all my sins. Lord Jesus Christ, today I give my life to you. I ask you to come into my heart and live in me and help me to live for you from today. In Jesus' name, Amen!*

Once you meant that prayer, Jesus Christ came into your life and He received your life. That prayer marks the beginning of your relationship with the Lord and positions you to live a life of victory over your storms here and prepares you for eternity with Him. Now, cherish that relationship and build it.

Maybe you are a reader who at some time in your past gave your life to Jesus Christ, but right now you know that you are not living for Him. You have drifted away from Him. Why not recommit your life to Jesus Christ today. Certainly, there is no better time than now to recommit your life to the Lord Jesus Christ. Please pray the following prayer of re-commitment and mean every word of it as you do.

PRAYER: *Lord Jesus I acknowledge you as the Saviour of the world and more importantly as my Saviour. I admit that I have been living to please myself and not you. I ask you to forgive me of my sins and my failure to serve you. Today Jesus, I recommit my life to you to live for you and serve you as my Lord and Saviour. In Jesus name, Amen!*

If you prayed that prayer, make a commitment to live for Jesus with everything in you from today and give Him the chance to do what He specializes in doing in your life. Your life will become fulfilling. You have no regrets when you live for Jesus.

CONCLUSION

Do you really want to defy the storms in your life and possibly make history at the same time? Then follow the principles outlined in this book and take action and see God come through for you.

The next time you get caught in a storm of life, look for a way to defy it and an opportunity to make history, if not for the world at least for yourself and those who know you. Show them how you can defy that storm in your life with the help of the Lord Jesus Christ. Peter used his storm to make history and so can you.

The Bible says, *"There hath no temptation taken you but such as is common to man: but God is faithful, who will not suffer [allow] you to be tempted above that ye are able; but will with the temptation also make a way to escape, that ye may be able to bear it"* (I Corinthians 10:13). In summary, this verse is saying that the temptations or trials in your life are not unique to you. Others experienced similar challenges and overcame them and so can you. It is unmistakably clear that God is faithful and He **will** make a way for you. When you surrender your life to serve Him, He will not allow you to go through a difficult situation that you cannot bear or overcome. This is one of the most encouraging verses in the Bible, and what it is saying to you is that whenever you face a storm in your life, God offers to help you and He will if you give Him a chance and cooperate with Him. Like Peter, take the way God makes for you and defy the storms in your life.

Bibliography

Douglas, J. D., N. Hillyer, F. F. Bruce, D. Guthrie, A. R. Millard, J. I. Packer and D. J. Wiseman, eds. *New Bible Dictionary*. 2nd ed. Wheaton. Tyndale House Publishers, Inc., 1982.

Edison Biography. Accessed 5th November 2018 https://www.nps.gov/edis/learn/historyculture/edison-biography.htm

Unger, Merrill F. *Unger's Bible Dictionary*. 3rd ed. Chicago: Moody Press, 1982.

Wafflesatnoon. *Was the only home to survive Hurricane Ike the site of a 1988 exorcism?* Available from http://wafflesatnoon.com/last-house-standing/

A small book for youths and singles dealing with the big issues of love, relationships and abstinence. It is both biblical and practical. Gives 10 practical ways to overcome sexual temptations.

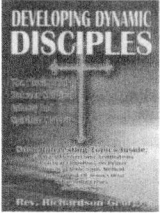

This is a discipleship workbook for new converts. It is written in a user friendly style with a very strong biblical emphasis and practical focus. There are 10 lessons. Also in Spanish.

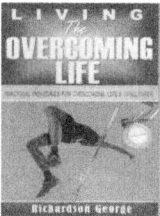

This book gives practical principles and strategies for overcoming life's challenges such as rejection, misunderstanding, unforgiveness, negativism, impatience, revenge to mention a few.

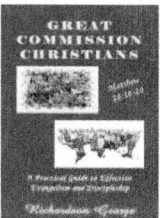

This book gives several practical strategies for personal and church evangelism. It spells out exactly how to do personal discipleship of new beliebers and gives a plan for church planting